J.C. PEPUSCH

Sonata in C major

for Flute (or Recorder), Oboe & Continuo

4 taps precede music

Edited by Virginia Brewer

Oboe

Adagio

4 taps precede music

Presto

Introduction to Ornamentation

Contemporary knowledge of style and practice in the 17th and 18th centuries is gained by studying a number of meticulously prepared treatises in the form of "tutors" or "methods" by the great teachers of the period. Certainly among the most valuable of these documents stands the "Essay of a Method for Playing the Transverse Flute" written by Johann Joachim Quantz in 1752. Having conscientiously lived through the tradition of the "High Baroque", Quantz was well equipped to preserve his first hand experiences and information for the edification of his contemporaries. The Essay, a giant of baroque musical literature, not only provides an excellent tutor for achieving technical mastery on the flute, but covers inexhaustible details of 18th century performance practice and taste.

Never preoccupied with the ideal of music for posterity, the baroque musician was primarily concerned with providing works for specific needs; music to be performed at the time, using whatever resources available to the occasion. Musical compositions were judged by their intrinsic qualities, the medium of performance considered quite secondary; therefore, alterations to suit the occasional need — instrumental substitutions, key transposition, abbreviations and extensions offered no serious concern to either performer or composer.

The overabundance of editorial markings dealing with dynamics, articulation and tempo to which the modern player is fettered were relatively foreign to the baroque manuscript, thereby inviting the tasteful and inventive performer to participate more intimately in the composer's efforts. In many instances scores were looked upon as mere suggestions or skeletons on which the musical essence could be enhanced and elaborated upon according to a traditional vocabulary of performance customs. The art of extempore, or spontaneous ornamentation on given notes or themes was as ordinary and commonplace as it was highly sophisticated, marking the baroque era as one of the most personal and eloquent periods of musical creativity.

Baroque ornaments may be explained in two classes: those categorized according to a prevalent system of signs, and those freely improvised. Fortunately for the historically aware performer, detailed ornamentation tables have been efficiently prepared by several old masters and one needs only to study the signs and their explication to arrive at the proper execution. In many cases, discrepancies of actual signs and terms appeared according to time and locale, but the basic method of delivery remained uniform. Several different tables of the most frequently used signed embellishments have been included to illustrate the minor points of discrepancy. Of these ornaments, the *trill* (basically an ornamented appoggiatura) is the most common and characteristic of the baroque, inspiring a wealth of written explanations as to its significance and appropriate handling.

— Shakes —

" Shakes add great lustre to one's playing, and, like appoggiaturas, are quite indispensable. If an instrumentalist or singer were to possess all the skill required by good taste in performance, and yet could not strike good shakes, his total art would be incomplete. While nature stands one person in good stead in this respect, another must learn the shake through much application. Some players succeed with all their fingers, some with only a few, and for still others the shake remains throughout life a stumbling-block presumably more dependent upon the constitution of the man's tendons than upon his will. With industry, however, many improvements can be made, if the player does not expect the shake to come by itself, and if, while his fingers are still growing, he takes the requisite pains to perfect it.

All shakes do not have to be struck with the same speed; in this matter you must be governed by the place in which you are playing, as well as by the piece to be performed. If playing in a large place which reverberates strongly, a somewhat slower shake will be more effective than a quicker one; for too rapid an alternation of notes is confused through the reverberation, and this makes the shake indistinct. In a small or tapestried room, on the other hand, where the listeners are close by, a quicker shake will be better than a slower one. In addition, you must be able to distinguish the character of each piece you play, so that you do not confuse those of one sort with those of another, as many do. In melancholy pieces the shake must be struck more slowly, in gay ones, more quickly.

Slowness or quickness, however, must not be excessive. The very slow shake is customary only in French singing, and is of as little use as the very quick, trembling one, which the French call *chevroté* (bleating). You must not be misled even if some of the greatest and most celebrated singers execute the shake chiefly in the latter fashion. Although many, from ignorance, indeed consider this bleating shake a special merit, they do not know that a moderately quick and even shake is much more difficult to learn than the very fast trembling one, and that the latter must therefore be considered a defect.

The *shake in thirds* in which the third, instead of the adjacent second, is struck above the principal note, although customary of old, and still the mode nowadays among some Italian violinists and oboists, must not be used either in singing or playing (except, perhaps, upon the bagpipe). Each shake must take up no more than the interval of a whole tone or a semitone, as is required by the key, and by the note upon which the shake originates.

If the shake is to be genuinely beautiful, it must be played evenly, or at a uniform and moderate speed. Upon instruments, therefore, the fingers must never be raised higher at one stroke than at another. "

All ornaments are played *on the beat,* the reason being twofold: to avoid rhythmic and melodic distortion, and to provide the spice of dissonance to a fundamentally consonant harmonic style. Quantz elucidates the 18th century thought on dissonance:

— Dissonance —

" To excite the different passions, the dissonances must be struck more strongly than the consonances. Consonances make the spirit peaceful and tranquil; dissonances, on the other hand, disturb it. Just as an uninterrupted pleasure of whatever kind it might be, would weaken and exhaust our capacities for remaining sensitive to it until the pleasure finally ceased, so a long series of pure consonances would eventually cause the ear distaste and displeasure, if they were not mingled now and then with disagreeable sounds such as those produced by dissonances. The more then that a dissonance is distinguished and set off from other notes in playing, the more it affects the ear. But the more displeasing the disturbance of our pleasure, the more agreeable the ensuing pleasure seems to us. Then the harsher the dissonance, the more pleasing is its resolution. Without this mixture of agreeable and disagreeable sounds, music would no longer be able now to arouse the different passions instantly, now to still them again. "

Regarding the addition of free improvised ornaments, Quantz provides ample suggestions of which a few are given here.

The player may experiment with these examples, in the appropriate places or invent his own as inspired from the style and character of each composition. In the use of both signed and improvised ornamentation, however, the performer is cautioned to use discretion as a guide and heed the following advice from Quantz:

— Extempore —

"Variations must be undertaken only after the plain air has already been heard; otherwise the listener cannot know if the variations are actually present. A well written melody which is already sufficiently pleasing in itself, must never be varied, unless you believe it can be improved. If you wish to vary something, you must always do it in such fashion that the addition is still more agreeable in the singing phrases, and still more brilliant in the passage work, than they stand as written. Not a little insight and experience are required for this. Without an understanding of composition, success is impossible. Those who lack the skill will always do better to prefer the invention of the composer to their own fancies. A long series of quick notes does not always suffice. They may, indeed, excite admiration, but they do not touch the heart as easily as plain notes, and this after all is the true object of music, and the most difficult one. Here also a great abuse has crept in. Therefore my advice is not to give yourself over too much to variations, but rather to apply yourself to playing a plain air nobly, truly, and clearly.

In general you must always see to it in the variations that the principal notes, on which variations are made, are not obscured. If variations are introduced on crochets usually the first note of the variations must be the same as the plain note; and you proceed in the same fashion with all the other values, whether they are greater or less than a crochet. To be sure, another note may be chosen from the harmony of the bass, but the principal note must then be heard immediately after it."

Source: In Playing The Flute
J. J. Quantz

G. P. TELEMANN

Sonata in C minor

for Flute(or Recorder), Oboe & Continuo

3 taps precede music

2 taps precede music

4 taps precede music

Andante

cantabile

8

Allegro

Fl.

MUSIC MINUS ONE • 43 West 61st Street • New York, N.Y. **10023**